SEWING

SEWING

HILARY MORE
SERIES EDITOR: ROSEMARY WILKINSON

SUNBURST BOOKS

Note: Imperial and metric measurements are not direct equivalents, so always follow only one set in a particular method.

This edition first published in 1994 by
Sunburst Books, Deacon House, 65 Old Church Street,
London SW3 5BS

Created and produced by
Rosemary Wilkinson and Malcolm Saunders Publishing Ltd
4 Lonsdale Square, London N1 1EN

ISBN 1 85778 047 7

Printed and bound in Hong Kong

Illustrations: Kate Simunek
Design: Ming Cheung
Cover photograph: Empress Mills (1927) Ltd, Empress Street, Colne,
Lancashire BB8 9HU

Contents

Introduction

Dressmaking is a skill that anyone can learn. Sewing can become a satisfying hobby, as well as being extremely useful for both your own and your children's wardrobe. Great pleasure can be gained from making your own clothes, new ideas and individual styles can be quickly created and you'll be saving money, too!

From the basic stitches and seams to the more complicated steps of adding zips, pockets and collars, this book will show you the easy step-by-step way to the perfect result. Each technique is covered and, with the help of clear diagrams, each method carefully explained.

Once the sewing is completed, there are tips on how to treat your clothes to keep them in the best condition.

Part 1:
EQUIPMENT

Measuring equipment

Tape measure
Essential for every sewing box. Choose a non-stretch tape measure with metal ends. Pick one with a combination of imperial and metric measurements. Tape measures are usually a standard 60in (150cm) length.

Yard (Metre) stick
A yard (metre) length of wood, used for marking long straight edges. Again choose one with both measuring systems clearly marked.

Short rule/ Sewing gauge
This short measuring rule, also called a sewing gauge, comes complete with an adjustable slider to measure a series of shorter lengths, such as button-holes and hems.

Cutting equipment

Dressmakers' shears
Large, strong scissors for cutting out the fabric pieces. They are available in various blade lengths, choose a standard 8in (20cm) size. The handles are bent up away from the blades so the fabric can be cut flat against the table.

General sewing scissors
Use these scissors for trimming seams and clipping off threads. With blades about 6in (15cm) long, the handles are straight.

Small sewing scissors
For snipping across buttonholes and sharp corners,

these handy scissors have sharp-pointed blades 4in (10cm) long.

Pinking shears
These shears cut a zigzag edge and should only be used for neatening seam allowances and not for cutting out fabric pieces as they will not provide an accurate edge.

Household scissors
Keep a pair of ordinary household scissors in the workbox for cutting paper patterns. Dressmaking scissor blades will be blunted if they are used for cutting paper and card.

Thread clippers
These clippers are held in the palm of the hand and used for clipping off threads.

Seam ripper
A U-shaped tool with a sharp curved edge is used to slice through stitched seams and to slash across buttonholes.

Rotary cutter
Combine this circular cutter with its special mat when cutting through several layers of fabric or paper. The cutter can be used by left and right-handed people.

Marking equipment

Dressmakers' carbon paper
Similar to office carbon paper, this paper is used in conjunction with a tracing wheel (see below) to

transfer guidelines from the pattern onto the fabric.
It is available in packets of different coloured sheets.

Choose a colour that will show up against the
fabric, then test a small piece first to make sure that
the marks will not show through to the right side of
the fabric.

Tracing wheel

A spiked wheel fitted on a wooden handle is
generally used with dressmakers' carbon paper.
Place the carbon paper between the pattern and the
fabric, then run the wheel over the guidelines of the
pattern to mark them onto the fabric underneath.

Tailors' chalk

Available in different colours to mark different
coloured fabrics, tailors' chalk can be brushed away
after stitching.

Marking pencils and pens

Modern alternative to chalk, check that the marks
will disappear or can be removed by washing before
using them on the fabric.

Pins

There is a huge range of pins available, each one
designed for a particular type of sewing.

Choose from steel, nickel plated steel, brass or
stainless steel. Match the pins to the fabric. The
standard pin is 1in (26mm) long, but 1 1/4in (30mm)
and 1 3/8in (34mm) lengths are also available in
some metals for thicker fabrics.

For fine fabrics use brass lace pins and pick ball-pointed pins when stitching knitted fabrics. Glass-headed pins are popular and useful when working with open weave fabrics. They are highly visible if accidently dropped on the floor.

Before you begin, check that the pins are sharp, blunt pins will snag the fabric.

Needles

Needles come in a good range of types and sizes. Match the correct needle to the sewing project. The higher the number, the finer the needle.

Sharps: In sizes 3-10, sharps are long needles used for tacking and gathering.

Betweens: Small sharp needles used for hand sewing, such as hemming. Available in sizes 4-10.

Straws: Very long sharp needles for stitching through several layers of fabrics and for gathering. Available in sizes 6-10.

Crewel: Sharp, medium-length needles mostly used for embroidery, such as smocking. They have long eyes for easy threading with thicker yarns.

Ball-point needles: Basically sharp needles with a rounded top, to prevent the needle from snagging knitted fabrics.

Bodkins: Short blunt or flat needles used to insert elastic and ribbon through casings.

Darning needles: Available in long or standard lengths, these needles are sharp with large eyes for darning yarns. Available in sizes 1-9.

Other sewing tools

Thimble

Essential for hand sewing, a thimble will help to push the needle through thick or difficult fabrics. Wear it on the middle finger of the sewing hand. Pick a steel thimble as silver ones are easily pierced.

Tape maker

This handy gadget folds fabric strips into ready-to-use bias binding. Available in three standard sizes, the fabric is fed into one end and pressed as it emerges folded from the other.

Beeswax

Run the working thread through beeswax to strengthen the thread when stitching on buttons.

Pin cushion

Keep pins handy by sticking them in a pin cushion. Pin cushions that fit on the wrist are also available.

Rouleau turner

A long metal stick with a catch at one end and a ring on the other, this helps to turn rouleau strips to the right side.

Needle threader

If you find it difficult to thread needles, use a fine metal threader, which slides through the eye and pulls back enclosing the thread.

Pressing

A good combined dry and steam iron and a clean
sturdy ironing board are vital for sewing. A sleeve
board and various pressing mitts can also be useful.

Sewing threads

There is a range of threads available for different
uses. Match the thread to the fabric.

Cotton thread: Smooth, strong thread with a
slight sheen. Use this thread on natural fabrics, such
as cotton and linen.

Mercerized cotton thread: A cotton thread
treated to make it lustrous and able to take a
coloured dye. Available in a huge range of colours
and in three thicknesses, use 40 for general sewing
and 50 or 60 for fine fabrics.

Polyester thread: An all-purpose synthetic thread
suitable for a variety of fabrics.

Cotton-wrapped polyester: Popular synthetic
thread, the polyester provides strength while the
cotton provides smoothness and lustre.

Silk thread: Strong and lustrous silk thread, not
only is used for stitching silks, but also is a bonus for
hand tacking fine fabrics, as it will not leave a mark
in the fabric when removed.

Tacking thread: Loosely-twisted cotton thread
that is easy to break, making it quick to remove
from fabrics.

Buttonhole twist: Can be either synthetic or silk, use buttonhole twist for topstitching as well as for buttonholes and sewing buttons in place.

Sewing machines

A must for the committed sewer, sewing machines come in a wide range of models. They are a worthwhile investment as, if regularly serviced, a sewing machine should last a lifetime.

Before you buy a machine, work out what type of sewing you need your machine to do. Almost every model will have the basic lock stitch and its variation, a zigzag stitch, so you can neaten edges and work buttonholes. More sophisticated machines can select different stitches and work complicated embroidery.

Sewing machines can be flat-bedded or free-arm. Free-arm machines mean that the area around the needle can be removed so you can stitch sleeves and cuffs and smaller children's clothes.

Another popular machine on the market is the overlocking machine or serger. These machines can neaten and finish garments in a professional way.

Sewing machine needles
Needles are available from 70/9 for fine fabrics up to 110/18 for thick fabrics.

Ball-point needles with rounded tips come in a range from 70/9 to 100/16 and are used for stitching knits and jersey fabrics.

Heavy jeans needles can be bought for stitching heavy-duty fabrics and wedge-shaped needles for stitching leather and suede.

For decorative work, double, and even triple needles can be fitted to most machines.

Fabrics

Fabrics are produced either from natural or man-made yarns. Yarn can be divided into spun yarn, which is made by twisting short fibres together into longer strands, and filament yarn which is a very long strand. All natural fibres, except silk, are spun yarns. Man-made fibres are filament yarns made from chemical solutions.

Fabrics are constructed by weaving, knitting, netting or bonding yarns together.

Woven fabrics

A good proportion of dressmaking fabrics are woven. Woven fabrics consist of a warp (lengthwise) thread through which a weft (crosswise) thread is woven. The tightly woven side edges are call selvages. There are many different patterned weaves such as twill, basket and pile weaves which result in a variety of fabrics.

Knitted fabrics

Knitted fabric is formed by a series of interlocking loops. This type of fabric has no grain but a rib is formed in the fabric to give it a lengthwise direction. Ladders can form in the fabric when one of the individual threads breaks.

Netting

Netting, which includes lace, is produced on special machines which try to imitate hand-made fabrics. The fabric has a main yarn outline held together by knots at the intersections. The mesh can vary from open to sheer lace.

Bonded fabrics

These are made from short lengths of fibre which are compressed and bonded together by steam. The main fabric in this group is felt.

Finishes

Most fabrics have some form of finish applied to them during or after construction. These finishes can alter the feel and properties of a fabric and generally make it more useful. Pre-shrinking, mercerizing and flame resistance are some of the finishes that can be added to a fabric. Decorative finishes that make the fabric look and feel better, such as dyeing and printing, embossing and glazing, can also be added to materials.

Natural fabrics

Natural fabrics are divided into cotton, linen, silk and wool.

Cotton

Cotton comes from the hairy seeds of the cotton plant. The fibres are strong and elastic, making cotton a strong and absorbent fabric – ideal for summer clothes and household items. Cotton can be easily and successfully printed but does crease badly and can shrink, however these problems can be overcome by mixing it with man-made fibres.

Linen

Linen comes from fibres of flax plant stems and is heavier and stronger than cotton. It is cool to wear and comes in many different weights from fine cambric to heavy slub linens. Linen creases, does not dye well and looses its crisp feel after washing. Again by mixing with man-made fibres, the bad qualities can be subdued.

Silk

Silk comes from the excretions of the silk worm which form a cocoon of silken threads. Some of the strands can be several feet (metres) long. Silk is strong and absorbent, it is crease resistant and drapes well, and is a marvellous fabric for clothes as it dyes well. However it must be washed at low temperatures or dry-cleaned.

Wool

Wool comes from sheep, goats, camels and rabbits. The fibres are woven or knitted together to form the fabric. Wool has tremendously absorbent properties, is crease resistant and elastic. Wool is also easily dyed. Wool is not a strong fibre and it will shrink when washed but these properties can be cured by adding man-made fibres.

Man-made fabrics

This term refers to all chemically made fibres. Man-made fibres can be sub-divided into fibres which are made totally from chemicals and fibres which are made up from natural substances, such as cellulose.

The best fabrics nowadays are made from a blend of natural and synthetic fibres which when mixed together form good quality fabrics containing the required properties.

Interfacing
This bonded fabric is held behind the main fabric to strengthen and support it. Interfacing can be sewn or fused (bonded) to the wrong side of the fabric. Interfacing comes in several different types and weights to match up with most fabrics.

Part 2:
TECHNIQUES

Hems

Narrow hem

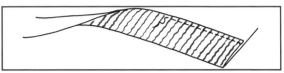

Turn under ⅛in (3mm) of fabric to the wrong side and machine stitch in place.

Double hem

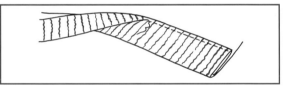

Turn under half the depth of the hem and press, then fold over the remaining half of the hem. Pin and stitch by hand or machine.

Seams

Points to remember before seaming:

★ If the fabrics are slippery or if you want to match the pattern exactly, tack the fabrics together before seaming.
★ Use a thread that either matches the fabric or is one shade darker.
★ Test before you machine stitch in case you need to change the size of the stitch.
★ Press all seams as you stitch them.

★ Begin and end with a few stitches worked in reverse to hold the threads firmly in position.
★ Place the bulk of the sewing on the left of the machine needle for smooth sewing.
★ Always take a seam allowance of $5/8$in (1.5cm) unless otherwise stated.

Plain flat seam

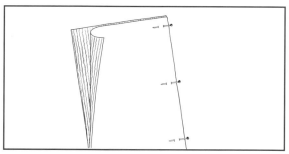

1 Place the two fabrics with right sides together, raw edges level. Pin horizontally across the seamline placing the pins approximately 3in (7.5cm) apart. Tack together alongside the seamline if necessary (see above).

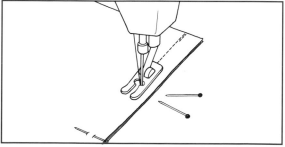

2 Stitch down the seamline, working a few stitches

in reverse at each end of the seam. Remove the
tacking stitches. First press the seam allowance to
one side, then press the seam open.

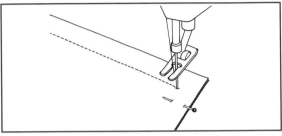

3 To stitch around corners, stitch up to the corner
point, then, leaving the needle in the fabric, lift the
presser foot. Pivot the fabric to line the needle up
with next edge. Lower presser foot and continue
stitching the next edge.

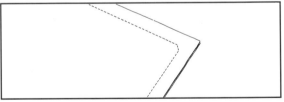

On heavier fabrics, work a couple of stitches
diagonally across the corner point, to help gain a
sharp point.

Neatening a plain flat seam
Simply use pinking shears to trim down each seam
allowance.

On lightweight fabrics, turn under the raw edge
and topstitch.

On heavier fabrics, oversew down each raw edge by hand or machine stitch over the raw edge using a zigzag stitch. Alternatively, fold bias binding in half over the raw edge and machine stitch in place.

French seam

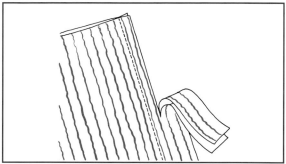

1 Place the two fabrics with wrong sides together, raw edges level. Pin and stitch the seam taking ³/₈in (1cm) seam allowance. Trim down seam allowance and press.

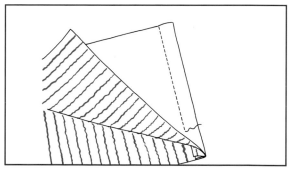

2 Refold the seam with right sides together so the seam lies exactly along the folded edge. Pin and stitch the seam again ¼in (5mm) in from the folded edge, thus enclosing the raw edges.

Mock French seam

1 Place the two fabrics with right sides together, raw edges level. Pin and stitch down the seamline. Trim down both seam allowances to ½in (1cm).

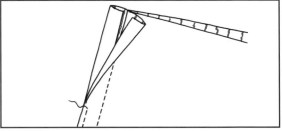

2 Turn in and press in ¼in (5mm) along both seam allowances, so the cut edges are enclosed inside. Pin and stitch together down folded edge. Press seam to one side.

Flat fell seam

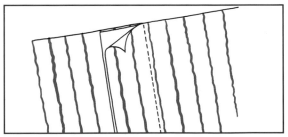

1 Place the two fabrics with right sides together, raw edges level. Pin and stitch together down the seamline. Press the seam open and then to one side.

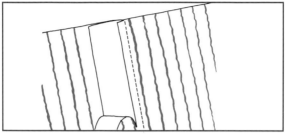

2 Trim down one seam allowance to ¹/₈in (3mm).

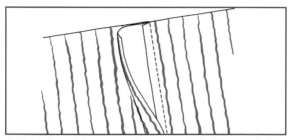

3 Fold the wider seam allowance in half around the narrower seam allowance and flat against the fabric.

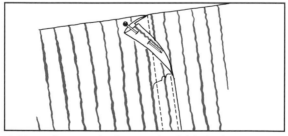

4 Pin and topstitch close to the folded edge.

Note: This seam could also be stitched from the wrong side.

Welt seam

1 Place the two fabrics with right sides together, raw edges level. Pin and stitch down the seamline. Press seam to one side.

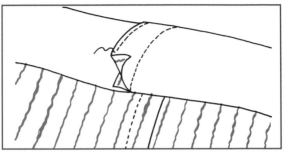

2 Trim down the inner seam allowance to ¼in (5mm). Topstitch wider allowance alongside the outer edge, thereby covering the narrower seam allowance.

Tucked seam

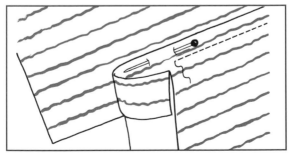

Press under the seam allowance on one of the fabric pieces. Place over the second fabric piece, aligning the raw edges. Pin and stitch down the seam ¼ - ⅜ in (5 to 10mm) from the fold.

Channel seam

1 Place the two fabrics with right sides together, raw edges level. Pin and tack down the seamline. Press the seam open.

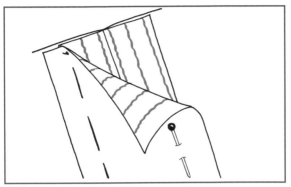

2 Cut a 1 ½in (4cm) wide strip of same or contrasting fabric. Centre the fabric strip under the pressed seam; pin and tack.

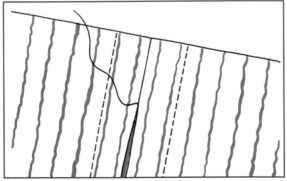

3 Topstitch down both sides of the seam an equal distance from the seamline, catching down both the seam allowances and the backing strip. Remove the tacking stitches.

Curved (Princess) seam

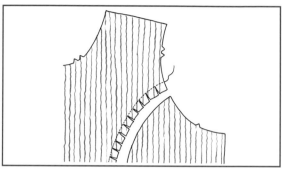

1 Staystitch around the inner curved edge just inside the seamline. Snip into the seam allowance up to the stitching line.

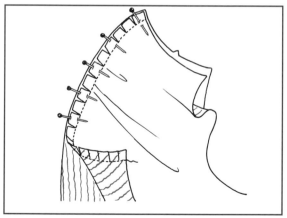

2 Place the two pieces with right sides together, raw edges level. Pin the inner curved edge on top and spread out the snipped edge to fit the outer curve.

3 Stitch together along the seamline; keep checking that there are no tucks in the stitching line.

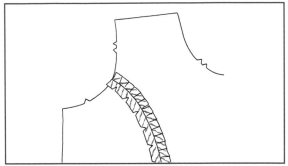

4 Cut out small triangles of fabric from the seam allowance on the outer edge to allow it to lie flat. Press the seam open.

GATHERING

Gathering fabric by hand

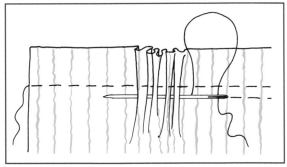

1 Thread a needle with a thread long enough to complete the gathering. Work from the right side. Begin with a backstitch. Work a row of fine running stitches on either side of the seamline, taking a few stitches on the needle at a time. At the end, leave the threads hanging free.

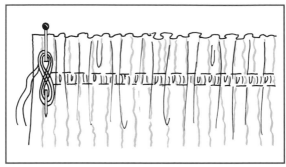

2 After working two rows, pull the threads up together until the fabric is the required width. To hold the gathering threads, place a pin vertically at the end of gathering and wind the threads in a figure of eight around the pin. Even out the gathers along the whole length. The gathered fabric can be stitched to hold the gathers in place before the seam is stitched. Remove any gathering threads that show on the right side after seaming.

Gathering fabric by machine

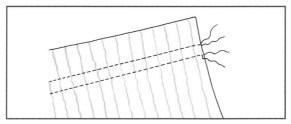

1 Work from the right side of the fabric. Set the sewing machine to the longest stitch and loosen the top tension. Work two rows of stitching, the first just inside the seamline and the second ¹/₄in (5mm) outside.

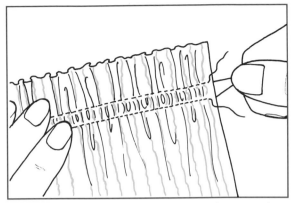

2 Pull up the two bobbin threads together to gather the fabric. Ease the gathers evenly across the whole width until the required measurement has been reached.

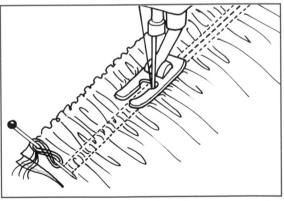

3 Pin the two fabrics with right sides together and wind excess thread around pin in a figure of eight, as before. Reset the sewing machine to a normal stitch and, working with gathered side uppermost, stitch the two fabrics together. Remove any gathering threads that show on the right side.

FRILLS

Single frill

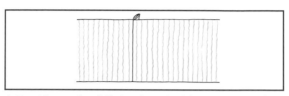

1 Decide on the frill depth and add 1in (2.5cm) for hem and seam. Cut out a strip to this width across the straight of the grain and to two to three times the finished length of the frill. If more than one strip is needed to achieve the required length, pin and stitch the strips together with a French seam.

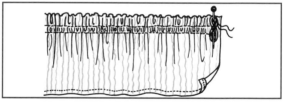

2 Turn up a double ¼in (5mm) hem along the base edge; pin and stitch. Work two rows of gathering stitch on either side of seamline, ⅝in (1.5cm) down from top edge. Pull up gathers evenly to the required length. Place a pin vertically at each end of the frill and wind around excess gathering threads.

On very long frills, divide up the fabric into sections and gather up each section separately.

Double frill

1 Decide on the frill depth and double it, then add

twice a ⅝in (1.5cm) seam allowance. Cut out a
fabric strip to this width on the bias and to two to
three times the finished length of the frill. If more
than one strip is needed to achieve the length, pin
and stitch the strips together with a plain seam.

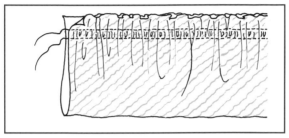

2 Fold the frill in half with wrong sides together.
Gather up the raw edge in the same way as before.

DARTS

Darts are marked on a paper patten by a V shape
bisected by a fold line. The V shape will have dots
at opposite points along both sides.

Stitching a dart

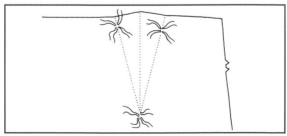

1 Mark the points of the dart position, with tailor's
tacks (see page 81), carbon paper or marking pencil.

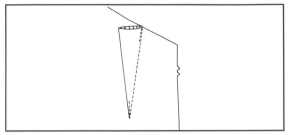

2 Fold the dart with right sides facing, matching points together; pin. Begin stitching at the widest part of the dart up to the point, then work a few stitches along the fold of the dart.

3 Press the dart to one side. If the dart is very big, cut along the fold to within ½in (1cm) of the point. Neaten the raw edges and press the dart open.

Tucks

Tucks are marked on a paper pattern by two parallel lines linked by an arrow. These lines are stitched together to form each tuck. Check that tucks are always folded on straight of the grain.

Pin tucks

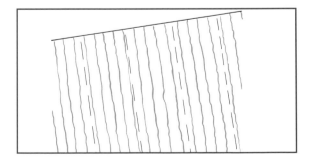

1 Mark the position of the tucks either with tailor's tacks (see page 81) or marking pen.

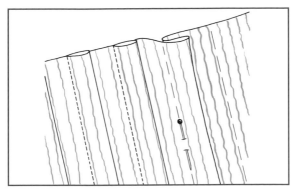

2 Form each tuck by folding the fabric along straight of the grain, bringing the first two sets of marks together. Pin and stitch down the tuck ⅛in (3mm) from the fabric fold.

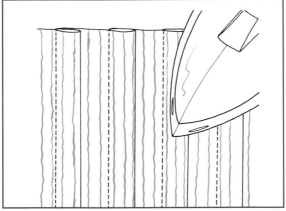

3 When all the tucks have been stitched, press the fold of each one to set the stitching, then press all tucks in the same direction.

4 Wide or spaced tucks have a flat area between each tuck.

Cross tucks

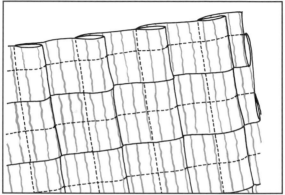

Cross tucking is a decorative way of stitching tucks. Mark and stitch all the lengthwise tucks first, as for pin tucks, then mark and stitch a second set of pin tucks at right angles to the first set. Check that all tucks are facing in the same direction.

Shell tucks

Shell tucks can be worked by hand or on a sewing machine that has the special facility of a shell hemming stitch. Each shell shape is usually twice the depth of the tuck.

1 To work by hand, mark and fold up the tucks, as for pin tucks. Thread a need with matching thread. Work a few running stitches along the seamline of the tuck, then take a stitch over the tuck itself.

2 Bring needle out on right side of fabric and take a back stitch following the line of stitching. Space shell tucks approximately ½in (1cm) apart along the whole length.

PLEATS

Pleats are a decorative way of disposing of fullness in a garment or fashion make. Use different coloured threads for marking the fold and place-ment lines on the fabric. Check that the pleats are folded along the straight of the grain.

Knife pleats

These are sharp concertina folds all facing in the same direction, although groups can be arranged to face each other.

1 Mark the fold and placement lines across the fabric. Mark the complete length of each line with tailor's tacks (see page 81) or marking pen.

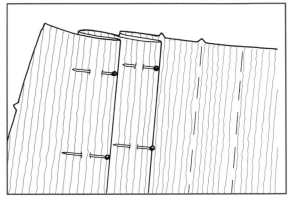

2 Fold the fabric along the first fold line exactly on the straight of the grain and position the fold over the placement line; pin to hold. Repeat, to pleat up each one in the same way, making sure that all pleats face in the same direction.

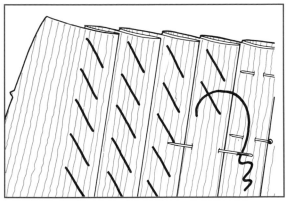

3 Diagonally tack down the complete length of each pleat.

4 Pin and stitch across the top of pleats following the seamline. Press the pleats well, sliding a piece of paper behind each pleat to prevent the fabric from being marked.

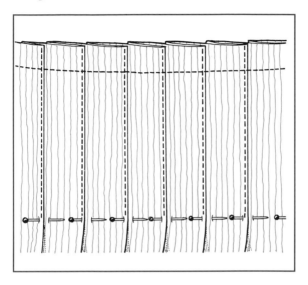

<u>Topstitching knife pleats</u>
To topstitch knife pleats, mark the end of the stitching with a pin. Topstitch down each pleat ¼in (5mm) in from the fabric fold. Fasten the thread ends on the wrong side.

Box pleats

These are made from pairs of knife pleats pressed away from each other, so that they form a box shape on the right side.

1 Mark the fold and placement lines as before: there will be two fold and two placement lines for each pleat.

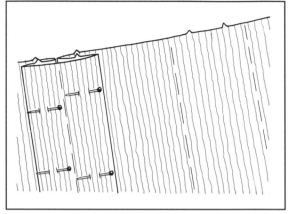

2 Fold along the fold lines and position along the placement lines as before, but forming the pleats into box shapes.

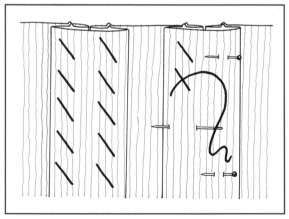

3 Pin and diagonally tack down the pleats as described for the knife pleats on page 38.

4 Pin and stitch across the top of the pleats following the seamline.

Part-stitching box pleats

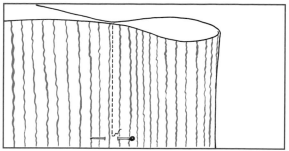

To part-stitch box pleats, mark the depth of the
stitching line on the right side, then, with wrong
sides together, stitch fold and placement lines
together down to the mark. Press the fold flat,
centred over the stitching line.

Topstitching box pleats

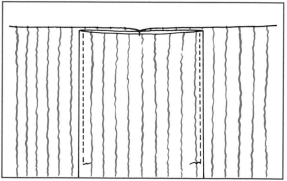

To topstitch box pleats, mark the depth of the
stitching line on the right side. Work a couple of
stitches across the base of each pleat, then continue
stitching up the pleat edge ¼in (5mm) in from the
fabric fold to the top.

Inverted pleats

These are made from pairs of knife pleats which meet together on right side. They are reversed box pleats.

1 Mark the fold and placement lines as before: there will be two fold and one placement line for each pleat.

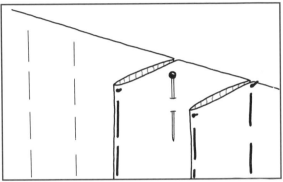

2 On the wrong side, match adjoining foldlines together; pin and tack.

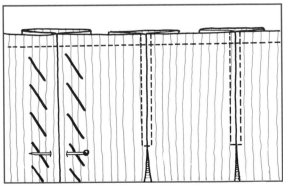

3 Place the centre placement line to centre of the

pleat; press well. Diagonally tack down the pleats
to hold. Stitch across pleats, as before.

<u>Topstitching inverted pleats</u>
To topstitch inverted pleats, stitch down one side of
centre fold, go across centre and up to the top edge
on the opposite side.

FACINGS

Neck facing

1 Cut out both back and front facings. Cut out the
same pieces from interfacing and fuse to the wrong
side of each fabric piece.

2 Place the back and front facings with right sides
together; pin and stitch the shoulder seams. Neaten
and press the seams open. Neaten the outer edge of
the facing either by zigzag stitching around the edge
or by turning under the edge for ¼in (5mm) and
topstitching.

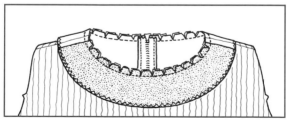

3 Place the facing to the neck edge with right sides
together and matching shoulder seams. Pin and
stitch together all around ⅝in (1.5cm) from raw
edge. Snip into the seam allowance around the
curved edges. Pull the facing up vertically and

understitch around the neck by stitching through both facing and garment turnings, as close to the seamline as possible.

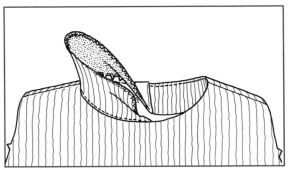

4 Turn the facing to the inside. If there are back edges, turn them under in line with the back opening; pin and slipstitch in place on either side of the opening. Work a few stitches by hand to hold the facing at the shoulder seams.

Combined neck and armhole facing

1 Complete the garment, leaving the shoulder seams unstitched. Cut out back and front facings. Place with right sides together; pin and stitch the side seams. Trim, neaten and press open.

2 Turn under ¼in (5mm) all around the lower edge of the facing; pin and topstitch or zigzag stitch over the raw edge.

3 Match the facing exactly to the garment with right sides together and neck, armholes and side seams all together. Turn back the facing along the seamline on the shoulder seam.

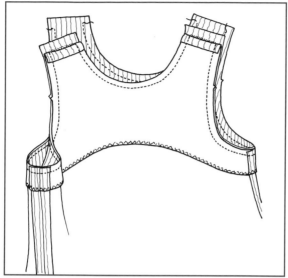

4 Pin and stitch around the neck, then around each armhole, beginning and ending the stitching at shoulder seams. Trim and turn the facing to the inside.

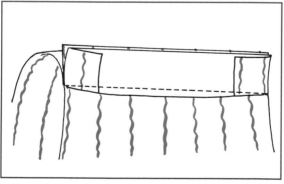

5 Place the shoulders of the garment with right sides together; pin and stitch. Trim and press open.

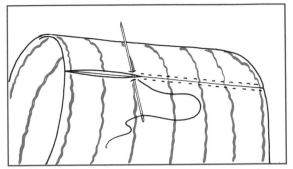

6 Slipstitch the folded edges of the facing together over the shoulder seams.

COLLARS

Two-piece collar

1 Cut out upper and under collars. Cut out one collar from interfacing and fuse to the wrong side of the under collar.

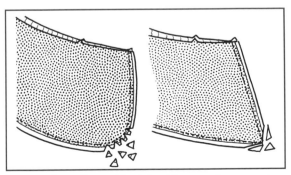

2 Place the collars with right sides together, matching outer and neck edges. Pin and stitch around the outer edge, leaving the neck edge open. Cut across the points on pointed collars and cut out small notches on the curved edges of peter pan collars. Turn right side out.

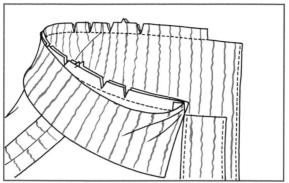

3 Before adding the collar to a garment with a front or back opening, finish the opening with a facing. Position the edge of the top collar only to the wrong side of the garment, matching notches and centre back or front. Pin and stitch to the garment. Press the collar up and the turnings to the inside.

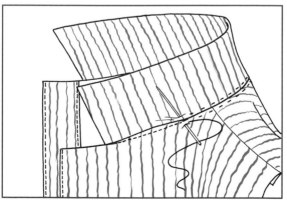

4 Turn under the remaining edge of the collar and slipstitch in place over the previous stitches.

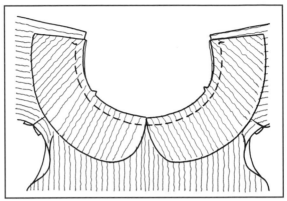

5 To attach a collar to a garment using a facing, make up the basic collar and tack the inner edges of the collar together. Place collar to neck, right sides together and matching notches with shoulder seams. Pin and tack. Neaten the outer edge of the neck facing.

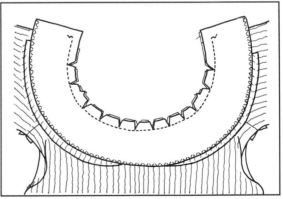

6 Place the neck facing over the collar with right side to right side of garment. Pin and stitch around the inner edge. Trim and clip into notches around the curved section.

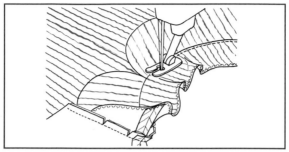

7 Turn fabric to inside and stitch through the facing and turnings only. Turn under the ends of the facing in line with the garment and slipstitch.

Shirt collar

This traditional two-piece collar has a collar combined with a small stand.

1 Make up the basic collar as before. Turn under the neck edge of one collar stand; pin and tack.

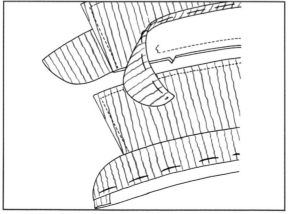

2 With right sides facing, sandwich the collar

between the two stand pieces, matching notches and collar ends to centre front. Pin and stitch together, continue stitching around the front ends of the collar stand. Turn the stand right side out and press.

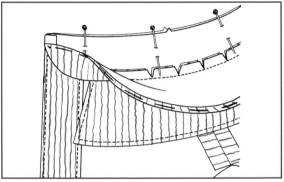

3 Place the untacked edge of the stand to the wrong side of the garment, matching notches. Pin and stitch in place. Trim and press turnings to the inside.

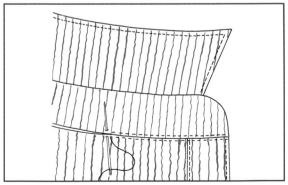

4 Pin and stitch the remaining folded edge of the stand over the previous line of stitches.

OPENINGS

Continuous opening

This kind of opening is commonly used on sleeves to accommodate the cuff.

1 Measure the opening and cut a strip of self fabric on the straight of the grain to twice the length of the opening by twice the finished width plus ¼in (5mm) for turnings.

2 Mark the line of the slit on the right side of the garment. Cut along the slit.

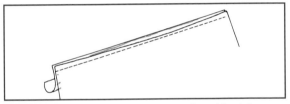

3 Place the strip centrally to open slit with right sides together and raw edges level. Pin and stitch, taking ⅛in (3mm) seam allowance. Taper the stitching around the slit end, i.e. in the middle of the strip. Press all turnings onto the strip.

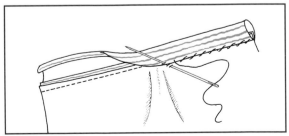

4 Fold the strip through centre to the wrong side of

the garment. Turn under the raw edge for ⅛in
(3mm) and slipstitch over the previous stitches.

Faced opening

This is also used on sleeves with cuffs.

1 Mark the position and length of the opening with
a line of tacking stitches. On a sleeve the opening
will be a quarter of the way in from the seam on
the back section of the sleeve.

2 Cut a piece of self fabric on the straight of the
grain, 3in (7.5cm) wide and the same length as the
opening plus 1 ¼in (3cm) for turnings. Turn under
¼in (5mm) on the side and top edges of the facing;
pin and stitch.

3 Place the facing to the sleeve, right sides together,
positioning the centre of the facing over the marked
opening line. Pin and stitch a scant ¼in (5mm) on
either side of marked slit, curving the stitching
around the top of the opening.

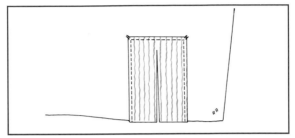

4 Cut carefully down the marked centre line. Turn the facing through the opening to the wrong side and press flat. Catch the facing to the garment with a couple of small stitches at each corner point at the top of the facing.

Box pleat opening

This opening can be used on necklines as well as sleeves.

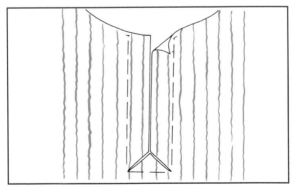

1 Mark the centre of the opening, then mark a line of tacking stitches half the width of the finished band on either side of the centre line. Cut down the centre mark to within 1/2in (1cm) of the end, then snip into each corner.

2 For the upper and lower bands cut two pieces, each twice the finished width plus 1 ¼in (3cm) by the length of opening plus 1 ½in (4cm). Cut and fuse a piece of interfacing, cut to the width and length of the opening, to the wrong side of each band.

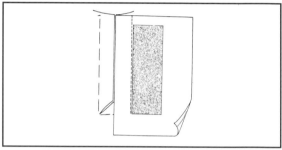

3 Place the right side of the lower band to the wrong side of the garment along the righthand side of the opening, matching top and side edges. Pin and stitch down the length of the opening following the staystitching. Trim down the turnings.

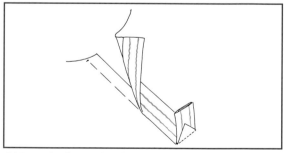

4 Turn the lower band to the right side and fold in half lengthwise. Turn under the raw edge at the side; pin and stitch over the seamline. With right sides together, stitch the end of the band to the garment across the triangle end of the opening, following the staystitching.

5 Pin and stitch the upper band to the opposite side of the opening in the same way, turning under the seam alowance at the bottom edge of the band and slipstitching together.

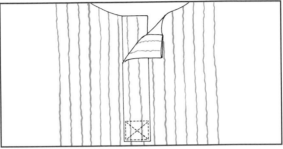

6 Place the upper band over the lower. Topstitch around the base through all thicknesses.

7 Add fastenings inside the band or add buttons and corresponding buttonholes.

8 The base edge of the upper band can be stitched into a point if preferred.

ZIPPERS

Edge to edge zipper

1 Pin and tack the complete length of the seam. Measure the length of zipper and mark this length along the seam. Stitch from this point to the base of the seam. Neaten the seam allowance and press the seam open.

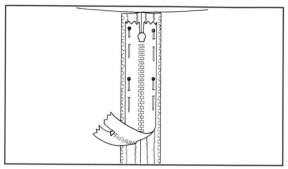

2 Place the zipper, right side down over the tacked section of the seam; pin and tack in place.

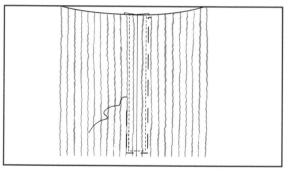

3 Turn the garment over and stitch the zipper in place following the tacked lines, using a zipper foot if machine stitching. Remove the tacking threads.

Lapped zipper opening

This is the best way to insert a zipper into a side opening of skirt or trousers.

1 Pin and stitch the seam up to the base of opening. Neaten the edges along the length of the seam. Turn under and press the seam allowance on the upper edge of the opening. This side will overlap the zipper; tack.

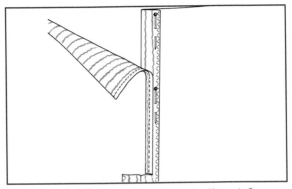

2 Turn under the opposite edge ⅛in (3mm) from the seam line. Snip into the allowance at the base point to release the edge. Tack down the folded edge.

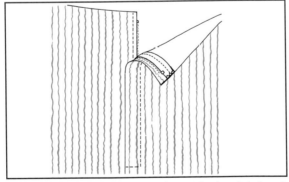

3 Pin underside folded edge alongside the righthand zipper teeth; stitch in place. Lay the lefthand side of the zipper to meet the edge of the seam allowance of the overlapping side; pin and stitch down along the line of tacking stitches and across the base.

Concealed zipper

1 Neaten the raw edges of the seam allowance. Mark the seamlines with a row of tacking stitches.

2 Open the zipper and place right side down on the right side of the garment, with the zipper teeth along the marked seamline and the tape over the seam allowance. Pin and tack in place.

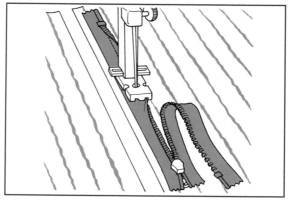

3 Fit a special foot on the sewing machine. Fit the groove of the foot over the teeth and stitch down as far as the tab. Repeat, to stitch the second side in place in the same way.

4 Close the zipper. Complete the garment in the usual way.

Fly-fronted zipper

This consists of a facing attached to the right trouser front and a flap to the left.

1 Tack down the line to mark the position of the

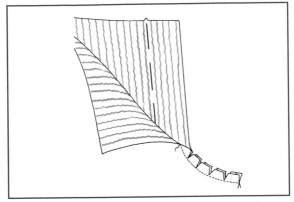

topstitching on the right front. Pin and stitch the trouser fronts together from the end of the zipper to the raw edge.

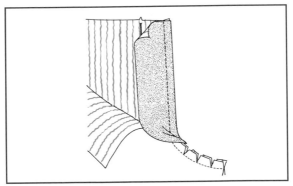

2 Cut and fuse a length of interfacing to the wrong side of the fly front facing. Place the facing to the right front, right sides together. Pin and stitch from the waist to the end of the zipper position. Press the facing seam open.

3 Place the zipper, right side down, over the facing with the lefthand side of the zipper aligned to the

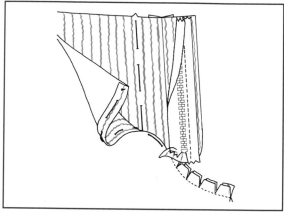

seam of the facing. Pin and stitch down the right-hand side of the zipper close to the teeth.

4 Turn the facing to the inside. Pin and tack in place. Topstitch following the tacked line. Turn under the left edge of the trouser front; pin and tack.

5 Open the zipper and place the fold edge of the left front over the zipper close to the teeth; pin and tack. Close the zipper.

6 Stitch the two flap pieces with right sides together. Trim and snip into the allowances. Turn right side out and press the seam to the edge. Turn the open edges to the inside; tack and stitch together. Place the flap to the wrong side of the left trouser front with the finished edge following the line of the topstitching; pin and tack.

7 Open the zipper; pin and stitch the lefthand side of the zipper in place through layers of trouser and

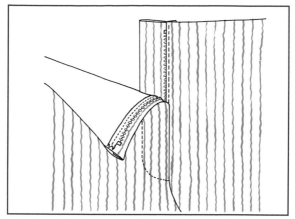

flap. Close the zipper and work a bar tack across the base of the opening.

BUTTONS AND BUTTONHOLES

Buttonholes can be worked on most sewing machines, following the handbook for instructions.

Hand-worked buttonholes

1 Use a tacking thread in a contrast colour to mark the centre of the garment. Measure and mark another row of tacking ⅛in (3mm) outside the centre line. Decide on the buttonhole length and measuring from the outside tacked line, mark another line down the garment.

2 Measure and mark the position of each button-hole horizontally between the tacked lines. Place the first one just below the neck edge and the last one approximately 3in (7.5cm) above the base of the garment. Space the remaining buttonholes approximately 3in (7.5cm) apart in between.

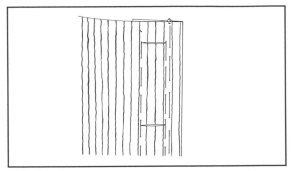

3 At each mark, slit the fabric along a single fabric thread between the two vertical tacked lines. Use a single thread in a matching colour to oversew all around the raw edges of the buttonhole.

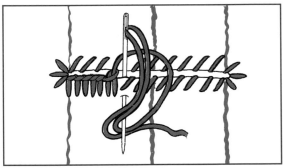

4 Thread the needle with buttonhole twist. Knot one end and slide the needle in between the fabric and facing to hold the knot. Beginning at the inner tacked line, work buttonhole stitch along the edge with ⅛in (3mm) long stitches fitted side-by-side. Check the edge is even and the knots are pulled so they sit along the cut edge.

5 At the outer edge, fan out the stitches around the end, then continue down the opposite side. On the

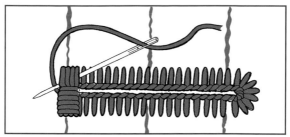

inside edge, work a set of vertical stitches across the complete width of the buttonhole. Cover these stitches with closely-worked blanket stitch.

When working vertical buttonholes, finish both ends with a vertical bar.

Bound buttonholes

1 Mark the vertical and horizontal tacked lines as before. Cut a piece of matching fabric for each buttonhole 1 ¼in (3cm) larger all around than the buttonhole.

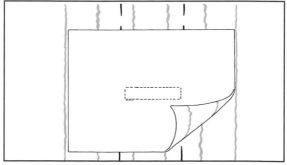

2 Place a fabric patch centrally over the first marked position, right sides together. Pin and stitch around the marked buttonhole position ⅛in (3mm) from the tacked line. Overlap the stitches along the base edge.

3 Cut through the tacked centre line to within ⅛in (3mm) of ends then cut diagonally into each corner.

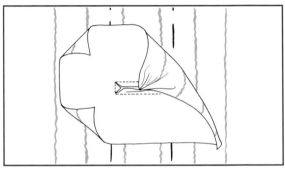

4 Press the sides of the fabric and push the patch through the centre slit to the wrong side.

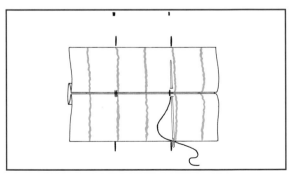

5 Fold the patch so that it forms two even strips that fill the centre slit; tack together. On the wrong side the fabric will form into small inverted pleats at each end. Hold these in place by oversewing the edges together at each side.

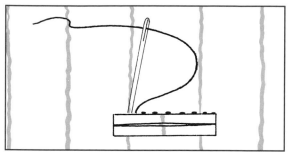

6 On right side, stab stitch all around the button-hole strips in the ditch of the previous stitches.

7 Repeat at each buttonhole position. Fold the garment facing over the buttonholes and tack around each one. Cut a slit along one fabric thread of the facing over the first buttonhole and diagonally into each corner as before. Use the point of the needle to turn under the facing edges all around the buttonhole; slipstitch the edges all around.

Button loops

1 Measure the diameter of the chosen button, this will be the length of the base stitches.

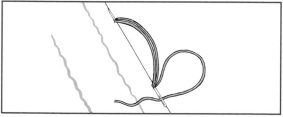

2 Thread a length of matching cotton and fasten into the garment edge. Take four stitches of the required length along the folded edge.

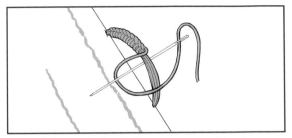

3 Work buttonhole stitch over the combined threads until completely covered. Fasten off.

Sewing on buttons

Buttons without a shank

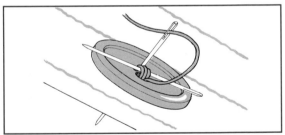

1 Sew on buttons without a shank using a double thread. Lay a thick blunt needle over the centre of the button and work the stitches over the top. Take the needle to the underside of button.

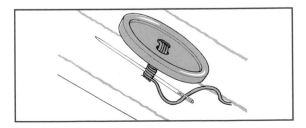

2 Remove the large needle. Pull up the button and wind the thread two or three times around the stitches securing the button. Take the needle to the back of the fabric, then fasten off.

Buttons with a shank

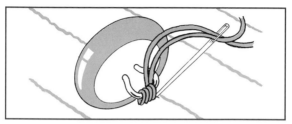

Sew on buttons with a shank with a double thread, working through the shank and fabric. Fasten off firmly at the back of the fabric.

OTHER FASTENINGS

Press fasteners

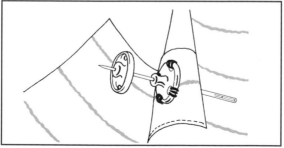

Sew the half with the ball to the underside of the top half of the opening and the socket section to the underside of the opening. Sew both halves in

position with three or four stitches through each of
the four openings. When the top half is in place,
push a needle or pin through the centre from the
right side to mark the position of the centre of the
socket section on the underside.

Hooks and eyes

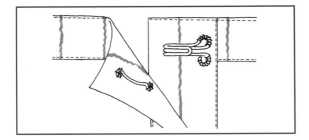

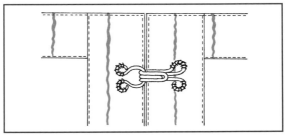

Fix a straight metal or thread bar when two garment
edges overlap and a round metal eye when the two
garment edges butt together.

Touch and close fastening

If using this type of fastening in strip form, cut to
the correct length and machine stitch in place on
either side of each strip.

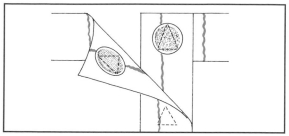

If using discs, stitch in place with a triangle of stitches.

SLEEVES

Set-in sleeve

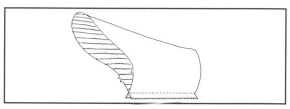

1 Fold the sleeve in half with right sides together and edges matching; pin and stitch the side seam. Neaten and press open.

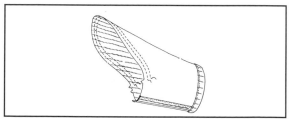

2 Finish the lower edge of the sleeve. Armhole placement positions are usually marked on one side of the sleeve with a single notch and on the other with a double. These are later matched to the body of the garment to fit left and right sleeves correctly. Work two rows of gathering stitches around the head of the sleeve from a single notch through centre top to a double notch, placing the rows on either side of the seamline.

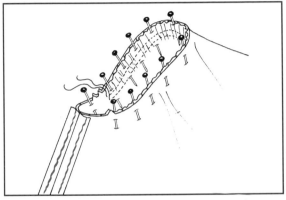

3 Fit a sleeve into matching armhole with right sides together. Pin the centre of the sleeve head to the shoulder seam and the side seams together. Match the notches on either side of centre to the notches on the garment. Pull up excess fabric on either side of the sleeve head to fit. Space out the gathers evenly. Pin and stitch in place, making sure that there are no tucks in the seamline. Overlap the stitching on either side of the side seam to finish. Neaten the raw edges as necessary.

Puffed sleeve

Work as for the set-in sleeve above, but stitch through gathers to produce the raised puff.

Raglan sleeve

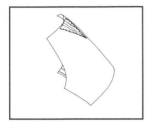 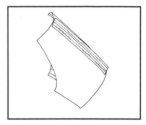

1 Pin and stitch the dart in the centre of the sleeve. Cut open and neaten the raw edges. Alternatively, if there is a seam instead of a dart, pin and stitch; neaten and press open.

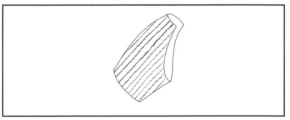

2 Fold the sleeve in half with right sides together; pin and stitch the underarm seam. Neaten and press the opening. Turn the sleeve right side out.

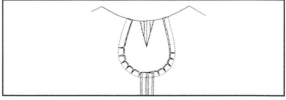

3 Matching underarm seams and neck edges, pin the sleeve into the armhole. Stitch in place. Trim and neaten the raw edges, snipping into the allowance around the curves.

Shirt sleeve

This sleeve is set into the shirt before the underarm seams have been stitched.

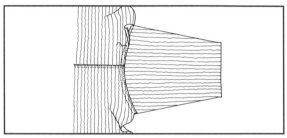

1 With wrong sides together, pin the sleeve into the armhole, matching notch to shoulder seam of shirt. Pin and stitch in place with a flat fell seam.

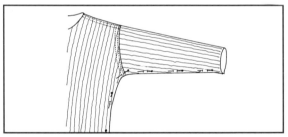

2 Fold the shirt so that the side and underarm seams match together. Pin and stitch from the wrist to the end of the shirt in one continuous flat fell seam.

Adding a cuff

1 Cut a one-piece cuff which is double the depth of the cuff plus seam allowances or two cuff pieces both the same depth as the cuff plus seam allowances. Fuse interfacing to one side of the one-piece cuff or to one cuff section.

2 Fold the one-piece cuff in half, wrong sides together; pin and stitch the side seams. Trim the corners, then turn right side out. Alternatively, seam two short and one long side of the two cuff pieces with right sides together; trim and turn right side out.

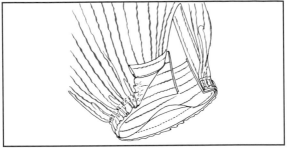

3 Place one edge of the cuff to the wrong side of the sleeve and pin at each end on either side of the opening. If the wrist is gathered, pull up the gathering stitches to fit the cuff. Ease out the gathers evenly along the cuff. Pin and stitch.

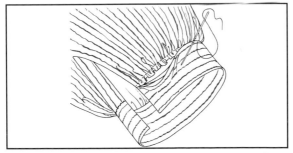

4 Press the cuff away from the sleeve. Turn under the remaining edge of the cuff covering the previous stitches; slipstitch in place, then add fastenings as desired.

WAISTLINES

Elasticated band

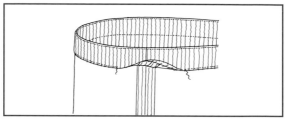

1 Measure a length of elastic around the waist, adding 1in (2.5cm) for the overlapping join. Turn under the waist edge for ¼in (5mm) then to the desired width of the band plus ¼in (5mm). Pin and stitch all around close to the edge, leaving an opening over a seam. Topstitch around the casing close to the top edge.

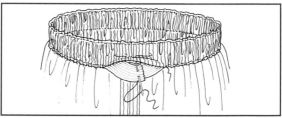

2 Fasten one end of the elastic to a safety pin and thread through the casing. Overlap the ends and stitch together firmly. Push the elastic inside the casing and complete the stitching to close the opening.

Stiffened band

1 Position the waistband to the garment with right

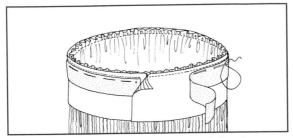

sides together and overlapping the ends by the
amount of the seam allowance. Pin and stitch. Cut
a length of waistband stiffening and tack to the
wrong side of the upper half of the waistband.

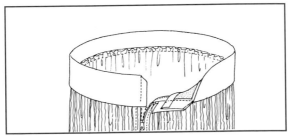

2 Fold the waistband in half with right sides
together; pin and stitch across the ends.

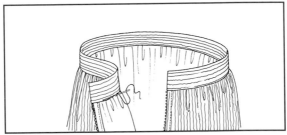

3 Trim and turn the waistband right side out. Turn
under the remaining seam allowance and slipstitch
in place.

POCKETS

Patch pockets

1 Cut out the pocket adding 1 ½in (4cm) to the top edge for the facing and ⅝in (1.5cm) seam allowance on the remaining edges.

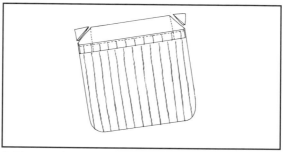

2 Turn under the top raw edge for ¼in (5mm); stitch. Turn the top allowance to the right side of the pocket along the top edge. Pin and stitch the sides. Trim and cut diagonally across the corners. Turn the facing through to the wrong side.

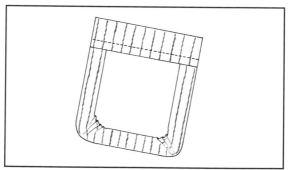

3 Turn under the remaining raw edges all around the pocket, pleating the curved edges where necessary; press flat.

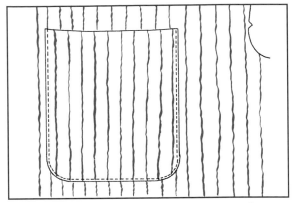

4 Position the pocket to the garment; pin and top-stitch in position.

Lined patch pockets

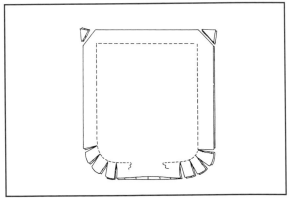

Patch pockets can also be made up with a lining; cut a lining the same size as fabric pocket. Place with right sides together; pin and stitch all around, leaving an opening in the base edge. Trim and turn right side out. Close the opening. Position and top-stitch to the garment in the usual way.

Pocket flaps

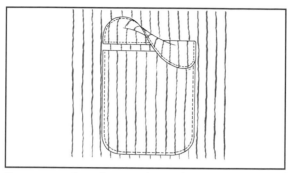

Separate pockets flaps can be made up in the same way and stitched above a patch pocket.

Concealed pocket set in a seam

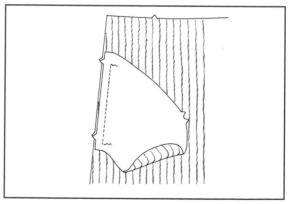

1 Cut out the front and back pocket sections. Position the front pocket section to the garment front with right sides together and matching any notches. Pin and stitch. Repeat to stitch the back pocket to the garment back in the same way.

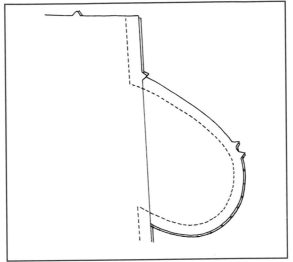

2 Place garment front to garment back with right sides together and raw edges level. Pin and stitch the side seams up to the marked position at the pocket, pivot the stitching and work around the pocket, then continue stitching the side seam in the usual way.

Part 3:
STITCHES

TAILOR'S TACKS

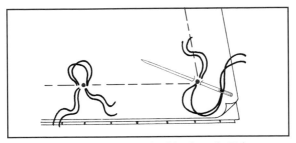

Thread the needle with a double thread. Take a
stitch at the marked dot on the pattern, leaving a
1in (2.5cm) long end. Take a back stitch in same
place, leaving a ³⁄₄in (2cm) loop. Cut off the thread
leaving a 1in (2.5cm) end. When all the tacks have
been worked, gently ease the fabric layers apart and
snip between each layer, leaving a set of marking
threads in each layer.

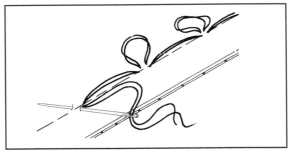

Tailor's tacks can be worked in a continuous line.

BUTTONHOLE STITCH

Work from left to right with the needle pointing in
towards the fabric. Fasten the thread with a couple
of backstitches worked on the spot. Insert the

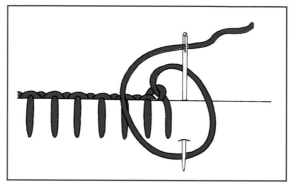

needle into the fabric behind the raw edge. Take
the thread from the needle and twist it around the
point. Pull the needle through so the knot falls on
the fabric edge.

BLANKET STITCH

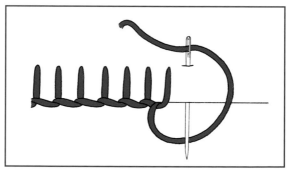

Work from left to right with the needle point facing
away from the fabric. Secure the thread end with a
couple of back stitches worked on the spot. Insert
the needle in the fabric from the right side and
bring it out under the edge. Pull the needle through
keeping the thread under the needle point.

Tacking (Basting)

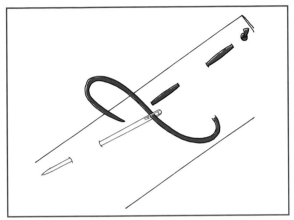

Work with either a single or a double thread. Tie a knot in the thread end. Work in and out of the fabric taking stitches approximately ½in (1cm) long. Keep the gaps between the stitches the same size.

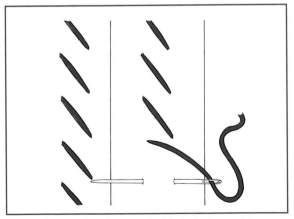

Work diagonal tacking to hold pleats in position (see page 38).

Running Stitch

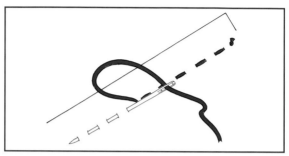

Work from right to left. Fasten the thread with a
couple of backstitches worked on the spot. Weave
the needle in and out of the fabric picking up a few
short stitches at a time.

Gathering Stitch

This is a running stitch made with a length of
thread as long as the line to be gathered. When
gathering, work two rows of stitches on either side
of the seamline.

Backstitch

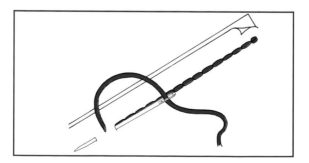

Work from right to left. Begin with a couple of
stitches worked on the spot. Work a running stitch
and a space. Take the needle back over the space
and bring it out the same distance in front of the
needle.

STAB STITCH

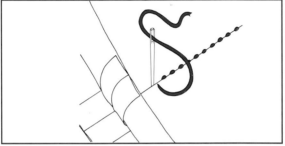

Work from right to left with the needle held in a
vertical position. Fasten the thread with a hidden
knot, then work along the seam taking tiny stitches.

OVERCASTING

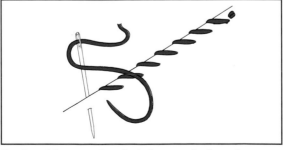

Begin with a couple of stitches worked on the spot,

then take evenly-spaced diagonal stitches over the raw edge. Work against the fabric grain and do not pull the stitches too tight.

SLIPSTITCH

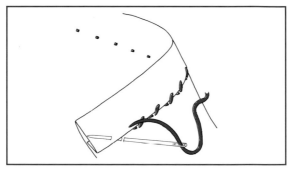

Hold the thread inside the hem with a knot. Work from right to left. Bring the needle out of the hem and take a tiny stitch in the fabric directly below the hem. Then take the same size stitch in the hem.

HEM STITCH

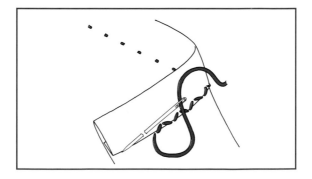

Work from right to left. Hold the thread in the
hem with a knot. Being the needle out of the hem
and take a tiny stitch in the fabric directly below the
hem. Then slide the needle through the fold of the
hem ready for the next stitch.

HERRINGBONE STITCH

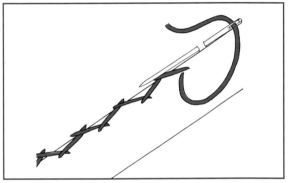

Work from left to right. Secure the thread with a
couple of backstitches. Bring the needle out of the
hem and with the needle pointing toward the left,
take a small stitch from right to left in the fabric just
above hem edge. Take the needle down ¹⁄₄in
(5mm) along and take another stitch from right to
left in the hem. Repeat, forming evenly-spaced
crosses over the hem edge.

Part 4:
CARE

WASHING

You can prolong the life of handmade garments provided you treat them with care and respect.

There is a universal range of standard care symbols for laundering garments and the aftercare needs of fabrics are often stamped along the selvages. The main symbols will tell you at a glance whether a garment needs to be dry-cleaned or whether it can be washed. The washing symbols are then sub-divided into different machine washable numbers and a hand washing symbol. Check before you use a washing machine that the garment can cope with this type of treatment.

When hand washing, only soak the garment in warm water mixed with detergent, do not rub. Squeeze out the excess water and rinse well before drying.

Before washing, check that all the pockets are empty, close zippers, buttons and other fastenings. Check that nothing has come loose and mend any holes and tears. Sort the washing into dark and light colours and wash them separately to prevent the light colours from becoming dingy. Divide all the garments by fibre content, so that all the fabrics can be washed at their correct temperature.

STAIN REMOVAL

Points to remember:

* Treat stains as soon as they occur.
* When using a chemical stain remover, treat the stain with a mild solution first before using the

remover at full strength to test how it reacts on the fabric.

★ When using a chemical stain remover, work around the outside of the stain in a ring, then work inwards.

★ Always work in a well-ventilated room and do not smoke when using chemical solutions.

★ Always test any chemical on a spare piece of fabric first, some solutions can damage the fabric or remove the colour.

★ Always remove a stain before washing a garment in case the washing sets the stain.

★ Keep chemical stain removers out of reach of children and pets.

★ Check if the fabric is washable. Most non-washable items will need professional cleaning to remove stains.

Useful products to keep at home

Bleach – use in dilute form to remove stains from white cotton and linen.

Borax – for acid stains on washable fabrics.

Enzyme (biological) pre-soak and washing powders – use to digest protein stains.

Glycerine – will help to soften stains making them easier to remove.

Household ammonia – for removing acid marks.

Methylated spirit – will help to remove residue colour from stains on colourfast fabrics.

Nail varnish remover – useful for removing adhesives.

White vinegar – use as an alternative to household ammonia.

Note: Before you try a chemical solution, blot or wipe away as much of the spillage as possible using a clean cloth or clean kitchen paper. Do not rub the mark. Try a rinse of cold water or soda water.

SPECIFIC STAINS
Adhesive

Treat clear and contact adhesive from the wrong side of the fabric. Soften adhesive with a pad soaked in nail varnish remover, then pick off. Wash or dry-clean.

Latex adhesive: can be removed while still wet with a damp cloth. If dry, use a specialist remover.

PVA adhesive: can also be removed with a damp cloth while still wet. If dry, rub neat washing-up liquid into the area before washing or dry-cleaning the garment.

Alcohol

Beer: mop up the excess with a clean, soapy cloth, then soak in warm water before washing.

Red wine: mop up the excess with a clean cloth. Place a sheet of clean kitchen paper under the stain. Sprinkle with salt, then rinse with warm water.

White wine: soak with soda water.

Soak stubborn stains in a solution of borax and water, one tablespoon of borax to one pint (600ml) of warm water.

On non-washable fabrics: sprinkle talcum powder on the area and leave to absorb, then brush off.

Blood

Blot off the excess with a clean cloth or kitchen paper. Soak with cold water and biological detergent. Avoid hot water which can set the stain. *On non-washable fabrics*: gently sponge with a solution of cold water to which a few drops of household ammonia have been added. Sponge with clear water to rinse.

Coffee/tea

Blot up the excess with a clean cloth or kitchen paper. Soak in a warm biological pre-wash powder solution. Wash in the usual way.
On non-washable fabrics: sponge with a borax solution, then with clear water.

Fruit/vegetables

Blot up the excess with a clean cloth or kitchen paper. Work neat washing-up liquid into the stain, then rinse.
On non-washable fabrics: use a borax solution.

Grass

Treat the stain from the wrong side of the fabric with a pad soaked in methylated spirit, or soak in a pre-wash solution.
On non-washable fabrics: professionally dry-clean.

Grease

When dry, scrape off the excess with a blunt knife. Use a solvent-based cleaner, then wash or dry-clean professionally.

Ink

Sponge with cold water before washing.
Felt-tip pen stains: sponge with a pad soaked in methylated spirit. Rub any remaining stain with hot, soapy water.

Ball-point stains: treat in the same way.

Make-up
Use a recommended solvent cleaner. Before washing, rub washing-up liquid into the stain.

Milk
Soak the stain in biological detergent overnight, then wash.
On non-washable fabrics: Apply a grease solvent .

Paint
Blot off excess paint with kitchen paper.
Emulsion and other water-based paints: should be removed by regular washing.
Gloss paints: dab with white spirit, then cold water. Wash in the usual way.

Perspiration
Sponge the stain with a pad soaked in a weak household ammonia solution.
On non-washable fabrics: sponge with a solution of white vinegar, then rinse gently with clean water.

Urine
Rinse the fabric under cold running water, then wash in the usual way.
On non-washable fabrics: sponge with warm salt water, then with clean water.

Index